JOB
BIBLE STUDY
BSBP SERIES
(Bible Studies for Busy People)

Margaret Weston is the author of 'How do I know I know God?' a best seller in Christian Evangelism and the first book in the 'How do I know?' series. She is also the author of the BSBP series. Full details can be found at www.howdoiknowbooks.com

All profit made by the author from this book is donated to Tearfund.

Tearfund is a Christian international aid and development agency working globally to end poverty and injustice, and to restore dignity and hope in some of the world's poorest communities.

Tearfund operates in more than fifty countries around the world. As well as being present in disaster situations and recovery through their response teams, they speak out on behalf of poor people on the national and international stage by petitioning governments, campaigning for justice and raising the profile of key poverty issues wherever they can. Find out more at www.tearfund.org

Copyright: 2012 Margaret Weston

ISBN-13: 978-1478349075
ISBN-10: 1478349077

BSBP SERIES - BIBLE STUDY
Old Testament - Job
CONTENTS

The BSBP Series   5

Background and Introduction to book of Job   6

Study   1 – Job's first test   8

Study   2 – Job's second test   12

Study   3 – Suffering   16

Study   4 – Eliphaz   20

Study   5 – Bildad   24

Study   6 – Zophar   28

Study   7 – Elihu   32

Study   8 – The Lord speaks   36

Study   9 – Epilogue   40

Study 10 – Conclusions   44

Reflections on Job   48

BSBP SERIES
(BIBLE STUDIES FOR BUSY PEOPLE)

The world is becoming increasingly busy and as Christians we are not immune from this. There always seems to be so much to do but so little time to do it! However, many of us love the Bible and would like to have more time to study it. So…………

The BSBP series has been prepared just for people like us – those who have a real desire to study the Bible but find they simply do not have enough time.

Do you want to study the Bible? Have you been put off by the length - and depth - of many of the books that are on offer? If your answer is 'yes' to these questions then the BSBP series is for you!

You will be taken step by step through your chosen book of the Bible - just 10 studies with 10 questions in each study. The brief supporting notes, will keep you focused on the job in hand. You will quickly and easily get a sound grasp of the subject matter - without having to use hours and hours of your valuable time!

These studies are ideal for both personal development and for stimulating thoughtful discussion within small groups.

The book of Job is a wonderful book which is challenging and yet encouraging and I hope you will enjoy using this study as much as I have enjoyed writing it! There are selected chapters and sections for you to read as you study this book. The idea of the BSBP series is to enable you to study without using too much of your time. However, if you can find time to read every chapter then this would obviously be of great benefit!

Full details of all the BSBP studies currently available can be found on the following website: http://www.howdoiknowbooks.com

May God bless you as you study His Word and by so doing increase in your knowledge of Him.

BIBLE STUDY FOR THE BOOK OF JOB
BACKGROUND AND INTRODUCTION

Why does God allow suffering? This question is asked so often by both Christians and non Christians and there is not an easy answer. Job had a problem with innocent suffering, and we do too, *because* we know that God is love. However, the book of Job does help us to understand some important principles surrounding this question of suffering. There are also many other lessons to be learned from Job including God's sovereignty; His right to do as He chooses; the need to trust Him even when we do not understand; and much more besides. We can also learn from Job's 'friends', in particular what not to say and do at such times! Job calls them, 'miserable comforters' (Job 16.2) and the expression 'don't be a Job's comforter' is used by many today even if they do not read the Bible.

Job is a particularly encouraging book when we are going through difficult times – but also when we are not! All of us, at some time in our lives, will have trouble. Jesus himself says, 'in this world you will have trouble' (John 16.33) so it is clear that becoming a Christian does not mean we will not have problems.

As we can see in the Bible study on James we can sometimes bring troubles and trials on ourselves because of our own behaviour or wrong choices. Job's 'friends' seemed to think that this had to be the reason for Job's suffering. However, sometimes trouble comes with no warning and not caused in any way by ourselves. We can be walking with God and leading righteous and godly lives and yet still we may experience terrible trials.

In the case of Job we see a man whom God called 'righteous' so it is clear that the problems he experienced were not his own fault even though his friends seemed to think this was so. His friends tried to explain his problems by using their own supposed wisdom and intelligence and by speaking *about* God, but Job finally came to acceptance and peace with God by speaking *to* God.

Job was a man of faith but in the midst of his suffering his faith was sorely tested and he rebelled against God. We hear of the patience of Job – and certainly he endured some very severe trials – but it was really God who showed patience as He listens to all Job's anger and questions for chapter after chapter. Eventually Job finds peace with God not in spite of his sufferings but *because* of them.

Things were going well for Job when suddenly, through no fault of his own, everything went wrong – very badly wrong. Can we still trust God through such times? Can we still have an assurance that He loves us? It is at such times that our faith is sorely tested. Peter says, 'these have come so that the proven genuineness of your faith – of greater worth than gold, which perishes even though refined by fire – may result in praise, glory and honour when Jesus Christ is revealed.' (1 Peter 1.7)

Many believe that Job may well be one of the oldest stories in the Bible, perhaps dating back as far as 2000 BC. However, the questions he asks and the lessons he learns are just as pertinent today as they were then. We know the same God to whom Job was speaking and with the guidance of the Holy Spirit we will be able to learn more about Him as we study this book.

Study 1 – Chapter 1
Job's First Test

Discuss/think about

When do you think your faith is strongest – when times are easy or when times are hard? Why might this be?

Read Job Chapter 1

1. What was God's evaluation of Job and what did Satan think of Job?

2. Do you think Job was aware of God's approval? Was he aware of the devil?

3. The book of Job was written a long time ago. How can we learn from the conversation between God and Satan so that it helps us now in our own lives.

4. Different people react in different ways when hardship/disaster strikes. What are these different reactions?

5. How would you react if all these things (verses 13-19) happened to you?

6. How did Job react?

7. As Christians do we/should we look at hardship differently to non-Christians? Explain how/why.

8. Job received all this terrible news and he 'fell to the ground in worship'. What would help us to hold on to our faith when trouble comes?

9. Read Ephesians 6:10-18. How does this scripture help us stand firm in troubled times?

10. Can you think of other scriptures which might also help when we have severe problems and trials in our lives.

Don't forget to pray!

Ask God for wisdom and understanding as we study the book of Job so that we can learn how to apply it to our own lives.

Notes for Job – Chapter 1
Job's First Test

For most of us it is probably true to say that our faith grows far more in difficult times than it does when things are going well. It is easy to forget God when everything is going well but it is when life is tough that we pray more and seek His presence. This is not always so of course and Job was an exceptional man. He was living a very prosperous life and yet he still feared God and shunned evil. He also interceded for his family lest any of them should curse God, the very thing that Satan would love them to do.

God was rightly proud of Job but Satan thought that Job's devotion was only because his life was prosperous and when the 'benefits' of believing were taken away then Job would no longer trust God. This is sometimes a charge against believers today and sadly with some it proves to be true. In the parable of the sower in Matthew 13 we see examples of those who fall away because the seed is not planted deep down in good soil. It is said that untested faith is immature faith but none of us really welcomes the testing!

Job does not seem to be aware of what was going on between God and Satan. In this book the original Hebrew refers to 'the accuser' rather than Satan and we know that Satan is always looking to accuse believers (Revelation 12:10). We do not understand much about the battle between good and evil but we do know that man's soul is the battle ground. One day we may understand the reason for our trials but for now we have to learn to trust God, irrespective of the circumstances. Can we love God because of who He is, rather than just because of His gifts? For many believers faith does not reduce the suffering but rather causes it. Job honours God here even when his circumstances seemed to deny the goodness of God.

We can react with bitterness and anger when trouble comes or we can allow ourselves to be softened and our characters formed by it. As Christians can we continue to believe that 'all things work together for good' (Romans 8.28) and that God has a good and perfect plan for our lives, even when it is not what we would choose for ourselves? Non-Christians do not have this anchor but even so we often see good coming out of evil in their lives e.g when they are motivated to help others who have experienced similar difficulties and so on.

We need to develop a close relationship with God when times are good, by constant prayer and reading of the Bible so that we are able to stand when the test comes.

Ephesians 5 gives us further insight into the battle between God and Satan. We know that God has already won the victory through Jesus and eventually Satan will be dealt with. In the meantime however Satan is allowed a certain amount of freedom. But even this is in accordance with God's plans and purposes, so that He can form us to be more like Jesus.

James tells us to 'consider it pure joy' when we have trials. Why? Because God is using the trial to change us and to bless us. 1 Peter 1:7 is another example - giving the example of the refining fire being used to test and strengthen our faith. There are many other scriptures too which speak about our faith being put to the test and it would be a good exercise to search for these.

Study 2 – Chapter 2
Job's Second Test

Discuss/think about

We will see in this next chapter that Job loses everything. Have you ever been overwhelmed by things that were happening in your life? Were you tempted to doubt the goodness of God or, if not, what kept you from doubting?

Read Job chapter 2

1. Why do you think God allowed this second test?

2. How do we see in this chapter that God is still in charge in spite of all Job's problems?

3. What do we learn about Satan from these first two chapters of Job?

4. Read 1 Corinthians 10:13. How does this relate to this passage? Does it help you to have confidence about the future?

5. How do you feel about Job's wife and the way she spoke to him? Why would this attack be dangerous to Job's faith?

6. How do you respond if you are challenged about your faith by someone who is very close to you?

7. Do you agree with what Job says in verse 10? How do you feel about accepting trouble from God?

8. What would help us to 'accept trouble'?

9. Do you think Job's friends helped him in this chapter?

10. How important are our friends when disaster strikes?

Don't forget to pray

Can we love God because of who He is and not just for what He gives us? Job's words show that at this stage he was prepared to do this. He was an extraordinary man and already we see God being proved right in His evaluation of Job and Satan proved wrong. We are in a more privileged position than Job and yet he had far more faith than most of us! Job lived in the time before Jesus came and died on the cross and rose again and before the Holy Spirit came to dwell in us. Ask God for a faith that wants to love and serve Him because of who He is rather than because circumstances are good or bad. Ask the Holy Spirit to help you trust God in every circumstance and to live a life which is pleasing to Him.

Notes for Job – Chapter 2
Job's Second Test

Of course we do not know fully why God allowed this second test. In the same way we do not fully understand why God allows testing in our own lives and the lives of those we love. Sometimes though we do have a little understanding either at the time of the trial but more often at a later date. We have already seen that Job seemed to be completely unaware of the conversation between God and Satan and he also seemed to be unaware that God held him in such high esteem. So far, Satan has got absolutely nowhere with God or with Job which is why he now proposes a far greater test – to destroy Job's health.

God knows though that Job will be able to stand this further test and we see that He is still in charge – see verse 6. God also knows what He is going to do in Job's life as a result of all he has to go through. We will see at the end of the book that Job is brought into a deeper relationship with God and will have a much greater knowledge of God as well as being given far more than he ever had before. So the recompense for Job will be both material and spiritual but of course he is completely unaware of this as he goes through this severe trial.

We learn from these first two chapters that Satan is a relentless foe and will constantly attack to try and tear us down. We also see that God allows certain things but He is always in control and can even use Satan to accomplish His own plan and purpose in our lives. God is the only one who can bring good out of evil and victory out of failure. We can find comfort in 1 Corinthians 10:13 which assures us that God knows what we can stand and will not give us more than we can bear.

Job's wife was a further test for Job. Often those close to us can cause us suffering. Job's wife appeared to have lost her faith and wanted Job to do exactly as Satan had predicted. There were two tests in these first two chapters – the first about the benefits of rejecting obedience to God and the second about the apparent uselessness of believing. Job refused to sin by cursing God and the issue is whether our faith is founded on personal gain or if it can be lost by personal loss. We can see similarities here with the temptations for Adam and Eve in early Genesis.

In verse 10 we see a marvellous justification for the reason God held Job in such high esteem. Satan must have been very angry to hear Job say such a thing. Already God has been proved right and Satan proved wrong and for the rest of the book we do not really hear anymore about Satan. However, in the following chapters we will see that God still continues to use the trial to teach Job and his friends more about Himself.

We need to make it a priority to deepen our relationship with God and allow the Holy Spirit to be free in our lives if we are to stand firm when trials come. We can do this by constant prayer, reading the Bible and bringing God into every area of our lives. If we know the Bible then God can use this to comfort us, strengthen us, guide us and help us – especially when trials come. If we do not know the Bible then it is more difficult for the wisdom in it to be brought into our minds by the Holy Spirit with the conviction that it is from God.

Study 3 – Chapter 3
Suffering

Discuss/think about

Have you ever felt angry with God because of what was/is happening in your life? Did you speak to Him about this, or speak to your friends or just keep it silently inside?

Read Job Chapter 3

1. Why should we always be honest with God about how we feel?

2. When you are in trouble do you find it easier to talk to God or your friends? Why?

3. How many 'why' questions did Job ask in this chapter?

4. Is it wrong to ask 'why' when trouble comes?

5. Who do you think Job expected to answer him? Who was the only person who was able to answer properly?

6. Job curses the day he was born but he does not curse God. What is the difference?

7. Read Jeremiah 20:14-18. Can you see any similarities with this chapter of Job?

8. What do you think is Job's greatest complaint or issue in this chapter?

9. How can you encourage or help someone who says they wish they had never been born?

10. Job pours his heart out to God in this chapter. Can you think of any other examples in the Scriptures where other people do this?

Don't forget to pray

Ask the Holy Spirit to help you to be completely honest with God. As a child with his/her parent, learn to pour out your heart to God at all times – whether you are happy or sad; in the good times and the bad. It is good to speak with friends but remember to speak to God first!

4   Youth
      bible

Notes for Job – Chapter 3
Suffering

We need to always be honest with God, not least because He knows us perfectly and already knows how we really feel! There is no use in pretending! However, we should also remember that our relationship with God will grow stronger and stronger if we develop the practice of always being honest with Him and pouring out our hearts to Him. He loves to hear from us and it is as we speak with Him, and sometimes even 'wrestle' with Him, that He will draw us closer and our relationship with Him will develop. We should try never to turn away and give Him the 'silent treatment' because if we do so we will lose the opportunity of learning more about Him which is always for our blessing.

Job asked many 'why' questions and we do too. In some ways he is taking up the case of the thousands who suffer through no direct fault of their own – those born into suffering situations e.g. refugee camps and poor countries. The question of innocent suffering is a huge one and asked by many people – Christians and non-Christians.

It is not wrong to ask God 'why' as long as we do not think that He owes us an answer. He is God and He is sovereign and has no obligation to explain everything to us. Even if He did there is much we would still not understand because of our limited intellect. As a parent cannot explain everything to the child so it is with God as our Father. Sometimes in His love and mercy God does explain a little that we are able to understand but it is only as we grow in our knowledge of Him and as our relationship deepens that we begin to understand more than we did before. Only when we are with Him eternally will we fully understand and in the meantime we have to have faith and trust in His love and His goodness.

Job was pouring out his heart both to his friends and to God but it was only God who could have answered his questions properly. Job cursed the day he was born but he is careful not to curse God which was the very thing Satan wanted him to do. We may not always like or understand what God is doing in our lives but still we can trust in His love and His goodness.

In this early part of the story of Job we can see that his friends did care for him and were willing to travel to be with him and sit with him in the ash heap. Probably they helped more at this stage by being silent and just 'being there' for him than they did in all the words they spoke in later chapters. Sometimes the best thing we can do for someone who is suffering is not necessarily to say anything at all, but just to be there for them and listen to their complaint.

Job's biggest complaint seems to be his lack of peace, quietness and rest (v26) and often when we are going through trials the greatest test of all is when we cannot find rest and peace for our souls in closeness to God.

There are other examples in Scripture of those who pour their heart out to God. We can see similarities with Jeremiah (see 20:14-18) and in Lamentations. Other examples are the Psalms and Isaiah. Abraham and Moses wrestled with God about what He was intending to do. We can see then that such conversations with God are the mark of those who are close to Him and not, as we might think, signs of unbelief or a lack of faith and trust.

Study 4 – Chapters 4, 5, 15, 16 and 21
Eliphaz

Discuss/think about

Can you think of a time when you were in trouble or going through a trial (or trials) and you were really helped by a friend? What was it that he/she said or did that really helped you?

Read the following sections of Job. There are a lot of scriptures to cover. These all relate to an ongoing conversation between Eliphaz and Job. If you are studying in a group it may be easier to choose two people from the group – one to represent Eliphaz and one to represent Job so that there is no confusion over which person is speaking.

Read Job (Eliphaz speaking) chapter 4:1-9 and chapter 5:8-18; (Job replying) chapter 6:14-17 and chapter 7:17-21

1. Why does Eliphaz think Job is suffering?

2. Is what Eliphaz says in chapter 4 verses 5 & 6 helpful?

3. Does Job find what Eliphaz is saying helpful or comforting?

4. Who do you think Job is speaking to in chapter 7:17-21?

Read Job (Eliphaz speaking) chapter 15:1-13 and (Job speaking) chapter 16:1-17

5. Can you see any change in the way Eliphaz now speaks to Job in this later chapter?

6. Why does Job now feel that both God and his friends have become his enemies?

7. Why do you think Job says that his 'prayer is pure' (verse 17)?

Read Job chapter 22:4-11 (Eliphaz speaking) and chapter 23:1-10
(Job speaking)

8. Eliphaz is now saying things about Job which are clearly
    untrue as we are told at the beginning of the book that Job
    was a righteous man. Why do you think Eliphaz feels he has
    to do this?

9. While Job does not yet know God (in the sense of having a
    personal experience of His presence) he knows that God
    knows him. Why is this such a comfort to Job and can also
    be such a comfort to us?

10. Why do you think that people sometimes seem to find God
    unresponsive even if they say they are seeking Him with all
    their heart?

Don't forget to pray

Ask God to show you how to be a true friend if\when someone you
know is in trouble.

Notes for Job – Study 4
Eliphaz

Instead of letting Job have his own experience and feelings Eliphaz tries to 'moralize'. His view is that sinners suffer therefore Job must have sinned badly to have all this trouble come upon him. It is not comforting or helpful to 'point the finger' at someone in trouble even if what we are saying is true. Eliphaz obviously had plenty of theology on which to lean but he seemed to be lacking in love and sympathy. He seemed to be trying to shame Job into silence rather than comfort him in his trouble. We are reminded of 1 Corinthians 13:2 – 'if I have all knowledge……but have not love I am nothing'.

Although Job was replying after his friend had spoken he was really speaking to God and continuing to pour out his complaint to Him. God's silence was causing him to go deeper in prayer and ultimately we will see he will be blessed because of this.

As Eliphaz continues to speak with Job throughout the book we find he becomes more aggressive and angry in order to try and get Job to listen to him – even to the point of saying later what is clearly not true about Job. He feels he has all the answers and is infuriated with Job for not listening to him. We need to take care when we are speaking with friends who are in trouble. We should not think we have all the answers because this will become apparent to our friend and be a real discouragement. Each person needs to work out their situation and problems with God on a very personal level and as we have already said, sometimes the less we say the better!

Poor Job feels that his friends have become his enemies because instead of helping him they are attacking him. He feels that God is attacking him and not hearing his complaint. He longs to be able to have a one to one conversation with God so that he can get answers for all his questions but God is, for the moment, remaining silent and hidden.

Job feels his prayer is pure perhaps because he is being totally honest with God and he is unaware of any sin that has caused all this trouble to come upon him. In spite of all he is going through and his discouragement at being unable to 'find' God he can still find some comfort from the fact that God knows him. We see that in spite of everything he is still trusting God, 'when he has tested me I shall come forth as gold' (chapter 23:10). God is still being vindicated in His approval of Job and Satan is still being shown to be wrong in his assumption that Job will turn away from God.

It should be a real comfort to us when we feel that God is distant from us that He knows us and will never leave us. In spite of how we feel we can cling to His promise that, 'I will never leave you or forsake you'. Psalm 139 is real comfort at such times. Sometimes God is silent in order to help us to persevere in prayer and to deepen in our desire to know Him. God's silence caused Job to begin to know more about Job and more about God and then eventually, when the time was right, we will see that God revealed Himself to Job in a wonderful way.

Study 5 – Chapters 8, 9, 10, 18, 19, 25-31
Bildad

Discuss/think about

Have you ever experienced a withering or judgmental attitude from someone when you were going through a very severe trial? If so, how did it make you feel? Or, if not, can you imagine how you would feel if this happened?

There are several scriptures to cover in this study. If you are studying in a group it might be helpful if you ask two different people to represent Bildad and Job in the readings.

Read Job chapter 8:1-6 (Bildad) and chapter 9:32-35 (Job)

1. Why did Bildad think that Job was suffering?

2. What do you think may have been the reason for Bildad's attitude to Job?

3. Bildad focused only on God's justice. What is wrong with this approach and what does it overlook about God?

4. How has Job's plea in chapter 9:32-35 been answered in Jesus?

Read chapter 18:1-5 and v21 (Bildad) and chapter 19:1-6 (Job)

5. Bildad was using sarcasm and fear to try and 'help' Job. Can fear be effective to help others?

6. What is the difference between the fear or reverence we should have for God in His almighty power and the fear that Bildad was trying to provoke in Job?

Read chapter 25:1-6 (Bildad) and chapters 26:1-4 and 27:1-6 (Job)

7. Bildad focuses here again on God's power and justice but do you think he really knew God?

8. Have you ever felt like responding with sarcasm as Job did in chapter 26:1-4 to someone who was offering you advice? Why was this?

9. Job said (chapter 27) that he didn't think God had treated him fairly. Do you ever feel that?

10. Can we sometimes be guilty of saying right things in a wrong way or with a wrong motive? If so how can we try to avoid this?

Don't forget to pray!

Father God help us to have sincere love for others so that when they need help we are able to help in a right way. Give us wisdom to know when to speak and when to be silent!

Notes for Job – Study 5
Bildad

Bildad thought that Job's suffering was Job's own fault and because of his guilt. We know this was not the case and even if it was it is not very encouraging to be told 'your words are a blustering wind' (8:2)! Job had poured out his grief and wanted sympathy but he did not find this in Bildad!

Bildad was so concerned about defending the justice of God that he forgot about the needs of his friend. We can sometimes say things that are right about God but if we say them at the wrong time and in the wrong way they can do more harm than good. This is particularly so if we do not speak in love and sympathy with the one who is going through the trial, for whatever reason.

Bildad focused on God's justice but forgot about His love and His mercy and His compassion. Bildad preached a sermon on the justice of God and whilst his theology was correct – God *is* just – his application was wrong in this situation. We have less excuse than Bildad for making this mistake, because we know that God's justice and His love were demonstrated and reconciled on the cross.

Job's plea in chapter 9:32-35 has been answered in the coming of Jesus. A mediator has been provided between God and man so that even though we are sinners we can be justified in the sight of God because of the death of Jesus on the cross. Jesus died on the cross for the sins of Job as well as our sins – "He is the atoning sacrifice for our sins, and not only for ours but also for the sins of the whole world." 1 John 2:2

Fear is a normal human emotion and there is nothing wrong with that as it is often used to keep us safe from danger. Fear of death and/or judgment is often a real and legitimate motive for putting our trust and faith in the Lord Jesus. Jesus himself says in Matthew 10:28 'fear Him who is able to destroy both soul and body in hell'. Jesus preached a message of love but also a message of judgment.

However, Bildad made two mistakes when he tried to use fear and the horror of death on Job. First of all, Job was already a believer and secondly he seemed to have a wrong motive for there did not appear to be any love in his heart towards Job.

We need to have a right fear of God and reverence towards Him. But because we know His love for us, we do not need to have a slavish fear of Him in the sense of being terrified. Bildad's speech in Job 25 is the shortest in the book and focuses on God's power and justice. It is interesting to see how Job's friends speak so knowingly about God but we shall see that, at the end of the book, God revealed that they didn't know what they were talking about! Perhaps we should be careful that sometimes it may be those who say the most about God who know the least about Him!

There is an important lesson to learn from Bildad which is that we can say right things about God to others, but if we do not have love in our heart towards them then we could cause a lot of damage. People who are hurting, for whatever reason, need love and can quickly spot insincerity. We need therefore to constantly ask God to give us love for others because we cannot manufacture it ourselves. It is only when we allow the Holy Spirit to work in us that we can show genuine love to others and thus know the right things to say, in the right way and at the right time.

Study 6 – Chapters 11, 12, 13, 14, 20, 21
Zophar

Discuss/think about

"How rarely we weigh our neighbour in the same balance in which we weigh ourselves" is a quote from Thomas A Kempis. Do you feel that you use the same balance for yourselves and others? Why/why not?

Read Job chapter 11:13-20 and chapter 20:4-7 and v28-29 (Zophar speaking)

1. We see from these verses that Zophar is now trying to 'help' Job. How would you feel if this message from Zophar was preached to you?

2. Zophar and his friends all operate on the assumption that sin produces suffering and that suffering therefore proves sin. What is wrong with this assumption?

Read Job chapter 13:5 and v15 (Job speaking)

3. What important lesson can we learn from verse 5?

4. What can we learn about Job from verse 15 that shows how wrong Satan was in his summing up of Job in the early chapters of this book?

Read chapter 21:7-16 (Job speaking)

5. What is the basis of Job's complaint in this section we have just read?

6. How do you feel about the fact that people who do not know or fear God seem to prosper?

7. Look at Matthew 5:45 – how do you think Zophar would respond to this? And how would Job respond?

8. How would you respond to the question in verse 15 if someone asked you this?

9. As the discussions continue in this book Job is moving away from considering his own experience of unjust suffering to a more general question. This general question is why there seems to be no correlation between doing good and being rewarded and doing evil and being punished. Have you thought/do you think like Job and if so what have been the results of your deliberations?

10. How can we help others to find answers to questions about the goodness of God?

Don't forget to pray

A good prayer to pray each day may be 'Lord help me today not to add to anybody's burdens.' Perhaps that should be our prayer too?!

Notes for Job – Study 6
Zophar

Zophar had a firm, but wrong, conviction that if anyone served God wholeheartedly and did not sin then they would not have trouble. Whilst much of what he says about 'the wicked' is right, it is linked wrongly to Job's predicament. The last thing Job wanted to hear as he sat on the ash heap in misery was someone telling him it was all his own fault! Job knew that bad things happen to righteous people as well as wicked people so these words of Zophar were not really of any help to him whatsoever. We know from our own experience that trouble comes to Christians and to non-Christians. John chapter 9 also makes clear that when we are suffering (the man born blind) it is not necessarily as a result of our own sin.

We learned from our study of James that there can be different kinds of trouble for the Christian and some of this can be as a result of our own behaviour or sin. However, we also have troubles and suffering simply because we are human. There is also the trouble which arises *because* we are Christians. Zophar was therefore quite wrong to emphasise the connection between sin and suffering to Job who was clearly a righteous man.

We can learn from Job 13:5 that sometimes the greatest wisdom is displayed by being silent! We do not know all the answers! Job 13:15 is a well known quote and is a tremendous expression of faith. "Job did not understand the Lord's reasons, but he continued to confide in His goodness" (C.H.Spurgeon). Oh to have faith like that! Once again God is proved right in his assessment of Job as we see Job continuing to trust God in spite of everything.

The basis of Job's complaint here was that he could see the wicked prospering and those who wanted nothing to do with God being able to live comfortable and prosperous lives. Even so, he says he wants nothing to do with them. His complaint against God is that such people are prospering while he, who does acknowledge God, is suffering. How often we see the same thing today! The Psalmist had the same dilemma – "this is what the wicked are like – always carefree, they increase in wealth' – Psalm 73:12. However, later the

Psalmist says 'when I tried to understand all this, it was oppressive to me till I entered the sanctuary of God; then I understood their final destiny."

As the discussions continue we can see that we are getting closer to the crux of the matter and the point at which the book began. What gain is there in serving God? If the righteous and the unrighteous both have blessings (rain and sunshine etc Matthew 5:45) and both have suffering, then why serve God? Satan said that Job only served God for profit and because all was going well. He said that if things went wrong for Job he would turn away from God. However, God knew His man and was shown to be right and Satan wrong.

The test for us is, can we still have faith in God and in His goodness even when things are not going well? Job was a wonderful man and did not have the benefits we have today. He is one of the few who God calls righteous. Today we can look at the cross of Jesus and know that if He loved us enough to die for us then that love can be trusted to always do the best for us – even if we do not understand sometimes what is going on. We also have the gift of the Holy Spirit who is a witness within us to the goodness and the love of God so that we can find the strength to continue to trust God even in the bad times.

Study 7 – Chapters 32-37
Elihu

Discuss/think about

We have been studying the suffering of Job and the response from his three friends. Think over all you have learned so far about how Job's three friends actually made the situation worse for Job rather than better. Do you think their intentions were good/bad? Were they just careless? Why do you think this happened?

At the end of chapter 31 we read 'the words of Job are ended'. He has finally exhausted all that he wants to say. We now move on to Elihu from whom nothing has been heard up to this point. Bible scholars have different views on Elihu but he does add something to the ongoing discussion and his speeches form a transition from Job to where God finally comes onto the scene and speaks. You will see a difference between Elihu and the previous three friends of Job and if you have time it would be good to read the complete chapters from 32-37. Job does not reply to Elihu and God does not mention him when He speaks of Job's three friends. For the purposes of this study we can only look at some parts of Elihu's speeches.

Read Job chapter 32:1–9 and verses 18-20; chapter 33:23-28; chapter 34:10-15; and chapter 36:22-33

1. Why had Elihu waited so long before he spoke? Why was he bursting to speak (32:19)?

2. Are you ever bursting to speak but you wait before doing so? If so, what reasons do you have for waiting?

3. Have you ever been helped by someone younger? How did you feel about this? Have you ever tried to help someone older than you? Was this easy or difficult?

4. In the passages we have read, what is Elihu trying to say about God? Why does he feel he must justify God? Do you ever feel like this?

5. Elihu was concerned to show God's justice. How do we reconcile the truth that God is just with the fact that this world is full of injustice?

6. Elihu speaks about God's greatness in terms of the creation and the way He controls it. What aspects of creation speak to you about God's greatness? Why?

7. Elihu stresses that God is in control, not us. How can this be a comfort as well as a stress factor when we are suffering?

8. How do you think you would have reacted to all that Job has been saying in this book?

9. We have covered 37 chapters and still God has not spoken into the situation. How do you react during times in your life when God appears to be silent?

10. How can you help others at such times?

Don't forget to pray

Father God, help us to cling onto your promises when times are difficult and you seem far away. Help us to remember that you have said 'never will I leave you; never will I forsake you' (Hebrews 13:5).

Notes for Job – Study 7
Elihu

In order to encourage others we need to seek to see things through their eyes. We also need to be humble enough to realise there might be other points of view. Job's three friends seemed to have quite a narrow experience of life and they were extremely dogmatic in their assumptions. What should have been an encouraging discussion among friends became quite a heated debate at times. When Job was going through so much, it was not the time for heated debate, even if the friends had been right - and they clearly were not. They said many false things about Job and assumed they knew the reasons for his suffering.

Elihu had listened throughout to all this and it seems that one reason he waited so long to speak was that he was younger than the other three. However, we can imagine that as he heard what was said he became more and more agitated until he could contain himself no longer. Sometimes the young ones are wiser than those who are older!

Elihu gave a very long speech – six chapters in all! During this speech he was explaining the character of God and applying this to Job's situation. Whilst some of what he said was similar to the others, his purpose was different. He was not trying to prove that Job was a sinner and somehow all his trouble was his own fault! He was trying to show both Job and his friends that their view of God was wrong. Elihu was explaining that God allows suffering not necessarily as a result of our sin, but to keep us from sinning and to make us better persons. We can see confirmation of this in the New Testament see 2 Corinthians 12:7-10 and Hebrews 12:1-11.

If you read the entire speech you will see that Elihu stressed many things and seemed to have a right view of God which Job's friends did not. Some important points are as follows; 1. God is gracious (Job 33:24); 2. God is just (Job 34:10-12); 3. God is great (Job 36:26).

We do need to say what is right about God but at the same time if we do not have love for those to whom we speak it will not achieve much at all – 1 Corinthians 13:2. We know that God is just but at the moment not everyone recognises Him as their Saviour and Lord and therefore may not be concerned about justice. Even those who do recognise God and are concerned about justice are weak and sinful and therefore the world is full of injustice. We know that 'each of us has turned to his own way' (Isaiah 53:6). As Christians we look forward to the day when justice will rule and 'every knee will bow and every tongue confess that Jesus Christ is Lord' (Philippians 2:10-11).

It is a comfort to know that God is in control of our lives and that in everything He is working for the good of those who love Him (Romans 8:28). However, the very fact that we are not in control can be a source of great stress to us unless we are willing to submit to God and trust Him for everything.

It is interesting to see that Elihu paves the way for God to speak. It is possible that while he was speaking an actual storm was brewing, because when he finished the storm broke and God was in the storm. He ends his speech reminding us that even though we cannot ever fully understand God, we do know that He does not allow affliction without purpose. There is a purpose and a reason for suffering even if we do not understand it. We have to learn to trust God even when we do not understand.

Study 8 – Chapters 38-41
The Lord Speaks

Discuss/think about

We will see in this study that God shows up at last! Share an experience you have had of being surprised by God. What life experiences have caused you to worship God?

Read chapter 38 and chapter 40:1-14

1. Is there a common theme in all the questions that God asks in these chapters?

2. Why do you think it may be more important sometimes in our spiritual journey to have more questions rather than answers?

3. Why does God remind Job about things he cannot do rather than things he can do?

4. What effect will this have on Job?

5. How does Job respond?

6. Why does God then continue to speak to Job?

7. Why do we complain against God either in our speech or in our thoughts? Or, if you never do complain against God then what prevents you from doing so?

8. In what ways do God's questions address Job's questions?

9. How do you feel as you read these words that the Lord said to Job?

10. Do you ever try to 'control' God? What would help us to learn not to try to do this?

Don't forget to pray

Oh Father God, teach us how we can increase in our knowledge of you. Help us to worship you for all that you are and not just for all that you do for us.

Notes for Job – Study 8
The Lord Speaks

Job had complained that he wanted to meet God face to face and argue things out with Him. However, when God did show up He asked a series of questions which Job had no hope of answering. The answer to Job's questions and problems was not an explanation about God which his friends had been trying to give him but a revelation of God. When Job finally met with God he found that he had nothing to say – there was nothing he could say in answer to all that God was asking. "I had a million questions to ask God; but when I met Him, they all fled my mind; and it didn't seem to matter." (Christopher Morley).

Francis Andersen comments on the aim of the Lord's speeches like this: "Their aim is not to crush Job with an awareness of his minuteness contrasted with the limitless power of God, not to mock him when he puts his tiny mind beside God's vast intellect. On the contrary, the mere fact that God converses with him gives him a dignity above all the birds and beasts, assuring him that it is a splendid thing to be man."

God's answer to Job and to us is not a theory or proposition – it is Himself. He invites us into a personal relationship with Himself, through the person and work of the Lord Jesus. Questions can be more important than answers sometimes because we need to be humbled in the presence of God and learn to submit to Him and to His will. We do not know everything and we cannot know everything. God is so far above us that there will always be more questions than answers (Isaiah 55:8-9).

God's enjoyment of His own creation comes through in His speeches and it is interesting to see that the creation is not just for man's enjoyment but that God also takes pleasure in it.

We might prefer God to speak to us in the sunshine but often He speaks in the storms in our lives. God spoke in the storm when He spoke to Israel on Mount Sinai (Exodus 19:16-19). Experiencing the greatness and majesty of God can humble us in a way that other things may not and in this instance the demonstration of God's power helped to ensure that Job was ready to accept the message God had for him. Job realised his own inadequacy and inability to meet God as an equal and defend his cause – even though he had been asking for this. Job's only response could be 'I am unworthy – how can I reply to you?'

However, it seems that although Job was silent he was not yet submissive or repentant. He knew he could not reply but God still had work to do in Him – often just like us! We can thank God that He does not give up on us or only partly complete His work but He always sees it through to the right conclusion – "being confident of this, that he who began a good work in you will carry it on to completion until the day of Christ Jesus." Philippians 1:6

We will see in the next study that God had more work to do in Job and finally Job comes to the place of repentance and submission before Him, acknowledging that whatever God does is right and man has no right to question it.

Study 9 – Chapter 42
Epilogue

Discuss/think about

Without intending to do so, Job has been condemning God and justifying himself (40:8). Are we sometimes inclined to do the same thing? Why/why not? We will see in this next chapter that Job is brought to real repentance. What does the word repentance mean to you?

Read Job chapter 42

1. What was the result of God continuing to speak to Job even after Job had come to the point of saying 'I am unworthy'? See chapter 40:3-6

2. What do you think Job means in verse 6 when he says he repents in 'dust and ashes'?

3. Repentance literally means a change of mind. It is not joyless self-hatred but a blessed God discovery. How can we ensure that our repentance is healthy repentance and not unhealthy self-disgust?

4. What do we now learn about God's evaluation of the different people in this story?

5. Why was God angry with Job's three friends?

6. What does Job now do for his friends that they should have done for him?

7. How has Job's attitude and relationship changed towards God as we come to the end of this story?

8. How do you think Job would now answer the question 'why are you, (or why am I) suffering?'

9. Do you think Job's three friends are changed as a result of this experience?

10. Why might Christians who are suffering find great encouragement in this book of Job?

Don't forget to pray

Ask God to help you understand real repentance and ask him to help you to deepen in your faith and trust in Him. Remember to pray for those who are suffering and ask God to show you how you can bless them and encourage them.

Notes for Job – Study 9
Epilogue

"There is a rebuke in this book for any person who, by complaining about particular events in his life, thinks he could propose to God better ways of running the universe than those God currently uses." – Francis Andersen

We are probably all guilty of thinking at times that we know better than God what should be done in our own lives and in the lives of others too. Repentance means literally 'a change of mind' and causes us to say yes to God and no to ourselves – to accept God's way rather than our own way. Throughout the book we see that Job refuses, quite rightly, to bow to the pressure of his friends and confess or repent of sins of which he is not guilty. He was a righteous man and was called righteous by God himself. He repents eventually of something more fundamental – thinking that he knows better than God; pretending he can think like God and of trying to play God.

Although Job realised his unworthiness when God first spoke he still had to come to true and full repentance which was why God, in his grace, continued to speak to him. Finally Job does repent 'in dust and ashes' – perhaps an indication of the depth of his repentance. Ashes were used to indicate deep grief at that time and we are made of dust – perhaps an acknowledgement of the fact that he is a mere man before a mighty God.

There is a difference between healthy and holy repentance and an unhelpful introspection which leads to self-disgust. We need to recognise the dignity that we have as being created in the image of God and yet have the humility of knowing that we are only creatures and God is God. The fact that God was speaking with Job gave him a tremendous dignity whilst at the same time causing him to repent of his pride in thinking he knew better than God.

We now learn God's view of Job and of his three friends. Job's friends spoke *about* God whilst Job spoke *to* God. We need to beware of having the right theology or the right knowledge in our heads which never reaches our hearts. Job was commended because although he complained and argued and wrestled with God he never gave up his faith. He had a real desire for a personal meeting with God and in the end God granted him that desire. His friends spoke about God and often said right things about God but it seemed to be without love and without knowing God personally. Just as the Pharisees often said right things, they had no love for those who were suffering and Jesus was similarly angry with them.

Job now prays for his friends and shows them by example the very thing they should have been doing for him! We see no bitterness towards his friends as he prays for them and God answers his prayer. He is no longer arguing with God and has accepted that what God does is always right – even if he, Job, does not understand it. He is still perhaps unaware of the reason for his suffering but he accepts that God does not have to explain what He does and is willing to submit. He now has a personal relationship with God and goes on to enjoy tremendous blessing for the rest of his life. Job came to know God in a way he would never have done if he had not gone through such an experience.

Study 10 - Job
Conclusions

Discuss/think about

What do we/you get out of having faith? Is it possible to love God and have faith in Him without expectation of reward in this life? How do you feel when/if you hear others speaking about the 'benefits' of following Jesus such as wealth, health, amazing experiences, if you have not had such 'benefit'?

1. If we reflect back to the beginning of the book of Job we should remember how it all started. Satan said to God, 'Does Job serve God for nothing?' In other words, he thought that Job would only keep his faith in God while things were going well. What have we learned now the story has come to an end?

2. Is it possible to love God and serve Him solely because of who He is, rather than for reward?

3. How has the book of Job helped you understand more about the big question of why people suffer?

4. Job is a wonderful book and there are many well-known verses found in it. Some of these are noted after the next set of study notes. Consider each of these verses and discuss what they mean to you personally. (If you are in a large group it may be easier to do this in small groups of three or four and take a couple of verses each.)

5. What is the most important thing you feel you have learned personally from studying the book of Job?

Don't forget to pray

Father God, help us to trust you even when we cannot understand what is going on. Help us to continue to walk by faith, knowing that

44

you will reveal your purpose at the right time. We ask that your Holy Spirit will spread your love in our hearts so that, whatever happens, we never doubt your love for us. Help us to live for you and to serve you while we are here on earth and to have joy in our hearts as we wait for the day when we will see Jesus face to face and be with you forever! Hallelujah!

Notes for Job - Study 10
Conclusions

There are many lessons to be learned from Job. He was an amazing man and one of the few in the Bible who are called 'righteous'. Yet, in spite of this, he had to endure the most terrible suffering. This is a very valuable book on the subject of suffering and shows that there are times when we do not know and cannot understand why certain people suffer as they do. Job never knew about the battle going on between God and Satan and we do not know what God is working out through suffering.

Sometimes of course we bring suffering on ourselves because of our behaviour or our sin but often this is not the case. It is those in the latter category to whom this book speaks great comfort. Suffering is seen almost as a privilege and a sign of God's love and esteem rather than as a punishment or even chastisement. God was vindicated in his evaluation of Job and Satan was defeated. Job showed that it was indeed possible to continue to have faith in God irrespective of the circumstances. Yes he was angry and rebellious, yes he argued and contended with God but he never lost his faith.

If we only have faith in God when times are good then perhaps we hardly have faith at all. If our faith is never tested we will never know how firm it is and yet we can take comfort in the fact that God knows us so well and will never put us through any trial for which we are unequal.

Two things are quite clear from the book of Job. The first is that good people do suffer and it need not be as a result of sin. The second is that we will never fully understand God's ways and should not expect to do so. God is God and has a right to do as He pleases without explanation. In His love and in His mercy he does sometimes give us wisdom to see why things are happening in order that we can learn from them. However, He is not obliged to do so and if He does not, then we know that we can still trust in His love. "He who did not spare his own Son, but gave him up for us all – how will he not also, along with him, graciously give us all things?" Romans 8:31

Another crucial lesson in the book is that of repentance. Without coming to a clear and deep repentance before God we will miss out on the reality of a personal relationship with Him. It is not just the sins we commit that should cause us to repent but we need also to repent about the pride within, which thinks it knows better than God.

The importance of knowing how to help others who are suffering is another lesson from this book. Those who are suffering do not need lectures on God and the causes of suffering, they need love and compassion and prayer.

Prayer is shown to be of the utmost importance in the last chapter as the Lord accepts Job's friends *as a result of his prayer*.

Finally, there are some amazing verses in the book of Job and only some of these are noted on the next page. During 10 short Bible studies it is impossible to fully explore all that Job has to offer but hopefully you will now be encouraged to delve deeper into this book at another time.

Reflecting on Job

Well-known verses from Job (NIV):

1:20   The Lord gave and the Lord has taken away; may the name of the Lord be praised.

7:17   What is man that you make so much of him, that you give him so much attention….?

9:2   But how can a mortal be righteous before God?

9:33   If only there were someone to arbitrate between us, to lay his hand upon us both.

13:15   Though he slay me, yet will I hope in him;

14:1   Man born of woman is of few days and full of trouble. He springs up like a flower and withers away; like a fleeting shadow, he does not endure.

19:25   I know that my Redeemer lives, and that in the end he will stand upon the earth.

23:10   But he knows the way that I take; when he has tested me I shall come forth as gold.

42:2   I know that you can do all things; no plan of yours can be thwarted.

42:5   My ears had heard of you but now my eyes have seen you. Therefore I despise myself and repent in dust and ashes.

Other Books by Margaret Weston

Margaret Weston is the author of the BSBP series and the 'How do I know?' series.

'How do I know?' Series

The 'How do I know?' series consists of an ongoing conversation between two people. The first book **'How do I know I know God?'** would be invaluable for you if you claim to be a Christian but are not sure whether you do have a personal relationship with God. It would also be helpful for those who have no faith and yet are intrigued by those who do. It is a best-seller in Christian Evangelism.

One of the reviews on Amazon.com says this about the book. "Every question you've ever had about God is considered in the light of what the Bible says. If you count yourself as a skeptic, I think you'll find every argument you've ever had with God will be resolved in this book."

'How do I know what God wants me to do?' is the second book in the series and is written as a challenge to the author herself and to Christians world-wide. Will you realise your potential in Christ? Will you take action - or if you are already doing so, will you continue to take action - to advance God's kingdom in our generation?

The third book in the series is **'How do I know God answers prayer?'** which is a question every Christian should be able to answer! However, the book also looks at the subject of prayer in a wider sense as the two unknown people continue to discuss this subject together. You will find questions that are often asked by those who know God and also those who do not.

BSBP Series

This series is intended to be for a specific group of people – those who really want to study the Bible but find they simply do not have the time. Life can be so hectic and whilst there are many very good

Bible studies and commentaries available, these can be quite off-putting for very busy people.

The studies do not claim to be an in-depth look at a particular book of the Bible. They are meant to be used as an overview and to help the reader obtain a good grasp of the subject matter without having to use hours of their time.

At the date of publication of this study the following studies are available in the BSBP series:- Ruth and Esther; Job; 1 Corinthians; James; Revelation Part 1 and Revelation Part 2.

Full details of all the books in both the **'How do I know?'** and the **BSBP series** can be found on the following websites. The books are all available from Amazon and selected bookstores.

http://www.howdoiknowbooks.com

https://www.amazon.com/author/margaretweston

Printed in Great Britain
by Amazon